D1708228

SUPREME COURT CASES

THROUGH PRIMARY SOURCES™

United States V. The Amistad

The Question of Slavery in a Free Country

David Hulm

rosen central
Primary Source™
The Rosen Publishing Group, Inc., New York

Published in 2004 by The Rosen Publishing Group, Inc.

29 East 21st Street, New York, NY 10010

Library of Congress Cataloging-in-Publication Data

Hulm, David
United States v. the Amistad: the question of slavery in a free country / by David Hulm.
   p. cm. — (Supreme Court cases through primary sources)
Includes bibliographical references and index.
Summary: This book discusses the Supreme Court's ruling of United States v.
Amistad, a case that put Africans on trial for staging a revolt aboard a slave ship.
ISBN 0-8239-4013-6
1. Cinque—Trials, litigation, etc.—Juvenile literature. 2. Trials (Mutiny)—United States—
Juvenile literature 3. Fugitive slaves—Legal status, laws, etc.—United States—Juvenile
literature. 4. Slave insurrections—United States—Juvenile literature. 5. Amistad
(Schooner)—Juvenile literature [1. Cinque—Trials, litigation, etc. 2. Trials (Mutiny).
3. Antislavery movements. 4. Fugitive slaves—Legal status, laws, etc. 5. Amistad
(Schooner)]. I. Title II. Series.
345.73'0231—dc21

2003005938

Manufactured in the United States of America

Contents

Introduction

In late August 1839, ships sailing around the eastern seaboard of New York City reported sightings of a mysterious schooner. The ship flew no flag and seemed to drift aimlessly. Most of its sails were in disrepair. Some people believed it was a ghost ship.

Some reported that the schooner was manned by savage black men, as high as fifty in number—some dressed like pirates, some half naked—and captained by a swash-buckling white man with a long white mustache. Others who had contact with the vessel and its crew met well-armed Africans desperately in need of food and water, willing to do nearly anything to get provisions. They accidentally frightened off those who could have helped them.

A U.S. freighter was sent to find this ship and question the crew but found no trace of it. Days later, during a chance meeting on a dune in Long Island, the histories of Africa,

Introduction

This watercolor painting by an unknown artist dates from the nineteenth century and is housed in the New Haven Colony Historical Society. The painting is titled, La Amistad, *and shows the Spanish ship as it might have looked when people first spied it in the northeastern shores of the United States.*

America, Spain, and Cuba would be forever changed by the discovery of the crew by two sea captains, Henry Green and Pelatiah Fordham, who were out hunting birds.

On August 26, Green and Fordham happened upon an unsuspecting bounty. As they rose over the edge of a dune, they met four black, mostly naked, African men. The two sea captains were impressed by the amount of gold jewelry worn by these Africans. The men, it seems, were willing to give all the gold to Green and Fordham in exchange for provisions and help sailing the damaged, barnacled, seaweed-strewn ship home to Africa.

Green and Fordham's eyeing of the gold begins the story of the legal battle for the ship, crew, and cargo of what would later be identified as the *Amistad*, a Spanish slave schooner taken over by Africans who had been captured and forced into slavery.

Almost as soon as Green and Fordham conceived the idea of claiming right of salvage of the *Amistad*, a U.S. Coast Guard brig named the *Washington* found and took control of the ship, capturing its crew. The lieutenants in charge of the investigation, Thomas Gedney and Richard Meade, determined that an uprising had occurred on the *Amistad*. After assessing the condition of the ship, they quickly decided they wanted to claim salvage rights as well.

The story of the mutiny aboard the *Amistad* is a drama that began in Africa nearly two hundred years before the characters in this story were born. In precolonial Africa, crimes were committed that would affect the course of human history. Some human beings were reduced in the minds of other humans to the status of property and merchandise. Laws reflected and reinforced the racist institution of slavery. Crimes of the most horrific nature were justified by both church and state.

Through time, bloodshed, and hard work, the world would eventually institute a unified policy against slavery. In addition, the world began to recognize basic human rights, not as a reaction against the "peculiar institution of slavery" but as a natural birthright.

A small part of the journey toward liberation involves the destiny of the Africans who took control of the *Amistad*. Their rebellion was the first step. However, attaining liberation would take a trial in the United States Supreme Court and the efforts of many lawyers, concerned U.S. citizens, a former U.S. president, and most important, the courage of the African slaves who asked to be simply and completely free.

A Mutiny Changes American History

1

Enslaved Africans traveled with Europeans to the so-called New World as early as the voyages of Christopher Columbus. In 1619, enslaved Africans arrived in Jamestown, Virginia, with European colonists.

By the time the *Amistad* set sail from Havana, Cuba, on the morning of June 28, 1839, an estimated twelve million Africans had been brought to the New World as slaves. On board the *Amistad*, forty-nine adult slaves and four children (three girls and one boy) were the "property" of Spaniards Pedro Montes and José Ruiz.

By 1839, most civilized nations had outlawed the importation of Africans as slaves into the colonies and countries of the Western Hemisphere. However, the institution of slavery was still legal in many nations and many U.S. states. The slave owners and traders aboard the *Amistad* were

United States v. The Amistad

American settlers in 1619 Jamestown, Virginia, view the arrival of the
first slaves to their colony in this painting by Howard Pyle. The work
was published in Harper's Weekly in 1917. African slaves were
brought to America to help build the new country as early as
Columbus's first voyage.

in violation of international law regarding the transport and ownership of slaves.

REBELLION!

On the third night of the *Amistad*'s voyage from Havana to its alleged destination of Guanaja, Honduras, Cinque, one of the enslaved Africans aboard, led a rebellion that resulted in the death of Ramon Ferrer, who was captain and owner of the *Amistad*, and the ship's cook. Fearing for their lives, two crew members jumped overboard. Two Africans were killed during the rebellion. Antonio, a cabin boy and slave owned by Ferrer, was spared his life.

Leader of the Amistad rebellion Cinque is the subject of this 1839 portrait by abolitionist painter Simeon Jocelyn. The painting is part of the New Haven Colony Historical Society. Cinque had been trained to be a leader of his West African village. But because he had not paid off a debt, he was captured by African tribesmen and sold into slavery.

Ruiz and Montes were spared because the Africans needed navigators. By day, the ship sailed east toward Africa, but by night while many of the Africans slept, Ruiz and Montes steered the ship north and west, away from Africa.

From the lack of good drinking water and from eating spoiled food, many Africans became sick—eight died—during the journey. When the Africans could, they would head toward land and attempt to gather food and drinking water. Their desperation drove them to search islands off the American coast in the hope of finding some guidance back to their homes in Africa. The *Amistad* was becoming less and less seaworthy. With torn sails and sea grass dragging along the bottom, the ship was barely able to navigate. Cinque was also concerned by the sight of so many sick Africans, weakened by their long journey.

DEATH BEFORE SLAVERY

When the sea captains Green and Fordham discovered the slaves, the Africans quickly offered much more gold than was necessary in exchange for help. And when the Africans returned to the *Amistad*, which had been boarded by U.S. Coast Guard lieutenants Meade and Gedney, they resisted arrest. For them, being captured again was not an option. As Helen Kromer writes in *Amistad: The Slave Uprising Aboard the Spanish Schooner*, Cinque was reported to have said, "You had better be killed than live many moons in misery." In their minds, they were free. They had fought for their freedom and won.

Cinque jumped ship and swam away from his captors on the *Amistad*. He was chased by some of Gedney and Meade's men and was finally captured. They returned him to the decks of the *Amistad*. On deck, Cinque pointed to the body of a dead African wrapped in a cloth. To his captors he said in his own tongue, "Here is a man who has found freedom."

Ruiz and Montes insisted on their fair share of the cargo. Both Spain and the United States claimed ownership of the slaves and cargo aboard the *Amistad*.

A Mutiny Changes American History

It was obvious to everyone that a crime or crimes had been committed. But the extent and nature of those crimes would take more than two years to determine and resolve. Among others, these questions remained:

- Who had committed the crime?
- When was the crime committed?
- Who could claim right of salvage of the *Amistad*?
- Were the Africans legally enslaved?
- Did the Spanish violate slave trade agreements?
- Were the Africans guilty of murder and theft?
- What role did the Cuban government play in the enslavement and transportation of these Africans?
- Who now owned or was responsible for the *Amistad*, its cargo (human and nonhuman), and crew?

Gedney took control of the *Amistad* and sailed it to New London, Connecticut. Connecticut was a state that had abolished slavery in 1784, but that legally held two dozen people as slaves. Here, he and Meade would have a much better chance to claim slaves and other cargo under right of salvage laws. Gedney informed U.S. officials of the successful capture of the *Amistad*. The ship had already become a legend. The two crew members who had abandoned ship during the mutiny had miraculously survived and swam to Cuba, where they reported the event.

Days after the capture by Gedney and Meade, an inquiry was held aboard the *Washington*. Ruiz and Montes had filed complaints against Cinque and the other Africans. They produced papers, signed by the governor-general of Cuba, giving permission to transport the enslaved Africans.

United States v. The Amistad

The Amistad Captives

After the Amistad slaves were captured and imprisoned, they were put on display for the interest and entertainment of Americans. This 1913 wood engraving, from a sketch drawn by Irving L. Hurlbert, shows a crowd watching some of the Amistad men put on a wrestling show.

The Africans were taken to jail in New Haven, Connecticut, to await a September 17 hearing in the district court. They were to be tried for murder and piracy.

JAILED

The imprisoned Africans became immediate celebrities. Their jail was also a tavern operated by a couple named the Pendletons. The Pendletons sold tours of the jail so that spectators could see the *Amistad* prisoners up close. At one time, as many as five thousand people paid between twelve-and-a-half

{ 12 }

and twenty-five cents apiece (about $2.27–$4.73 today) merely to walk past Cinque.

Merchants sold masks of the Africans' faces and engraved images, much like today's baseball cards. Around their cells in New Haven, a circuslike atmosphere surrounded the African prisoners. They were paraded around town, performing acrobatic tricks for the amusement of U.S. citizens.

Many of the African captives entered jail already feeling ill. Three died by mid-September. Mostly, they were afraid. They could not understand English or Spanish, and no one seemed to understand their languages. The little communication that did take place came through sign language. How were they to represent themselves in court if no one understood them? And under these serious charges, they would need a great deal of help.

Trials and Tribulations

2

Everyone seemed to want a piece of the *Amistad*. England, a country not even directly involved in the incident, was determined to punish any act of what it deemed to be piracy and mutiny. Like the U.S. government, England saw the *Amistad* mutiny as an act of murder and piracy. The high seas would not be safe if an act of piracy went unpunished. Although it publicly outlawed slavery, the British government urged the United States to try the *Amistad* Africans for murder and piracy.

In Connecticut, where the *Amistad* Africans were being tried, the action taken by the Africans against the Spaniards was considered illegal because slavery was still being practiced in parts of the state. As slaves, the Africans had no rights—especially not the right to murder their masters or plunder the cargo onboard the ship.

Gedney and Meade had another angle to pursue. Meade testified that he boarded the *Amistad* under the jurisdiction of the United States because Ruiz had asked him for protection. Because of a 1795 treaty (the Spanish-American Treaty of Commerce and Amity of 1795, known simply as the Treaty of 1795) signed by the United States and Spain, Meade was obligated to help Ruiz and Montes. Because the *Amistad* was considered a derelict ship (it was without captain and crew and in terrible condition), and because they had "discovered" and boarded the ship, they believed they had a right to its cargo. Slaves at that time were selling for more than $1,000 a person. If the claim held, Ruiz and Montes would be wealthy men.

Ruiz and Montes made separate claims for their rights to their slaves. The Spaniards argued that since the *Amistad* was a Spanish ship, the slaves were legally obtained and were their property, due to the Treaty of 1795.

Merchants in Havana also made a claim on part of the cargo of the *Amistad* since the ship had left Cuba with their merchandise on board.

Remember Captains Green and Fordham, the men who ran into the Africans on shore? They also claimed rights for salvage based on the fact that they had detained (held) some Africans on land while Gedney and Meade boarded the *Amistad*.

REAL EVENTS BECOME ENTERTAINMENT

Less than a week after their capture, plays were produced in New York that showed the story of the Africans aboard

This Civil War relic is a portrait of Wilson Chinn, a branded slave from Louisiana. It was taken by Kimball studios in New York City in December 1863. The photograph is now housed in the Library of Congress. At Chinn's feet lies a display of torture instruments that were used to punish slaves.

the *Amistad*. News stories around the country focused on the exotic rebels from Africa who challenged the institution of slavery.

Public opinion on the case was widely split. On one hand, there were those who saw the Africans as less-than-human, ignorant, murderous savages who had violently taken the *Amistad* to satisfy their blood thirst. On the other hand, there were those who believed the Africans had merely done what anyone else in their position might have done. Facing the horrifying reality of lifetime enslavement and loss of liberty, they argued, the Africans had fought back as best they could to return home to Africa.

The case of the *United States v. The Amistad* would mark a crucial turning point in the inglorious history of

The woodcut shown above, printed in 1807 in a book called The Penitential Tyrant, *depicts a slave wearing an iron mask and collar. Along with leg shackles and spurs, such inhumane devices were commonly used to punish and restrict slaves and force them to remain obedient to their masters. The woodcut can be found in the Library of Congress.*

slavery in the United States. Americans had long been aware of the contradiction between the brutal reality of slavery and what the Declaration of Independence called the inalienable rights of life, liberty, and the pursuit of happiness. Even those most often identified with notions of liberty, such as Thomas Jefferson and George Washington, owned slaves. How could a society that valued liberty so highly support the institution of slavery?

Because of the widespread publicity surrounding the *Amistad* case, abolitionists and sympathizers soon organized support for the Africans.

SLAVERY

An estimated twelve million Africans reached the slave auction blocks of the Americas. According to African American historian John Hope Franklin, half of those who left the slave holds of West Africa perished during the journey. Because the slaveholders were often in the minority, they used extensive methods of brutality to keep the Africans from rebelling. Torture, including rape, whippings, beatings, and the cutting off of limbs, was used to keep the slaves under control. As seen in Stephen Spielberg's 1997 film, *Amistad*, slaveholders often drowned slaves to maintain food supplies or to keep military vessels or pirates from claiming their cargo.

Slaves were chained in the holds of the ship, and never received medical care or sufficient food. They were not allowed to use bathrooms, so the slave holds (the places on a ship where slaves were "stored") often smelled like a combination of human feces, urine, sweat, and sickness. Before they arrived at the auction blocks, they were washed and fed by the slavers.

At the auction block, the enslaved were stripped naked, oiled, and poked and prodded like animals. Brutality continued for the rest of their lives. Once enslaved, few could ever look forward to freedom through their masters' hands. In a few instances, slaves were set free once they became too old to be productive. However, they had no way to support themselves once freed.

Trials and Tribulations

Sometimes slaves were freed when their masters died. Other masters allowed slaves to purchase their freedom. Often, the only way to freedom was through escape. Even if a once-enslaved person entered a "free" state, he or she could be caught and returned to the condition of slavery.

It was known as the "peculiar institution of slavery" because slavery obviously contradicted the notions of freedom and liberty on which the United States was founded, yet it was part of day-to-day life for nearly three hundred years. Although legislation after the Civil War ended slavery and guaranteed liberties for African Americans, it would take further amendments to the Constitution in the 1960s to establish full liberty and equality under the law.

A slave auction is depicted in the wood engraving above, which was published in the Illustrated London News *on September 27, 1856.*

FRIENDS COME TO THEIR AID

Abolitionists were those who felt, for many different reasons, that slavery was wrong and should be abolished (ended). Within the United States, abolitionist groups were divided. The *Amistad* case united them. What many abolitionists agreed on was that slavery was morally wrong; most felt that the *Amistad* case would help the abolitionist movement gain momentum. At this time in U.S. history, it was critical for the movement to become more popular in the North. Although slavery was illegal in most northern states, many felt that while slavery was wrong, abolition would cause racial turmoil.

The economy of the South depended on the institution of slavery and the survival of the United States depended on cooperation among the states. So, while many northerners were opposed to slavery, they did not publicly state their opposition. In fact, northerners who openly fought against slavery often found themselves physically attacked for their beliefs. It was dangerous to oppose slavery in the North as well as the South.

Abolitionists E. W. Chester (a lawyer from Connecticut), the Reverend Joshua Easton (a black abolitionist), Joshua Leavitt (a lawyer and editor of the *Emancipator*, one of the leading antislavery publications), Roger Baldwin (a well-known lawyer in the cause against slavery), Simeon S. Jocelyn, and Lewis Tappan (a New York merchant), came to the aid of the Africans. They formed what was called the Amistad Committee. There were others as well who demonstrated their support by raising money for the Africans' defense, by providing food and clothing to the Africans, and by arguing for their release.

AMERICAN
ANTI-SLAVERY
ALMANAC,
FOR
1840,

BEING BISSEXTILE OR LEAP-YEAR, AND THE 64TH OF AMERICAN
INDEPENDENCE.   CALCULATED FOR NEW YORK; ADAPTED
TO THE NORTHERN AND MIDDLE STATES.

NORTHERN HOSPITALITY—NEW YORK NINE MONTHS' LAW.
The slave steps out of the slave-state, and his chains fall. A free state, with another
chain, stands ready to re-enslave him.

Thus saith the Lord, Deliver him that is spoiled out of the hands of the oppressor.

NEW YORK:
PUBLISHED BY THE AMERICAN ANTI-SLAVERY SOCIETY,
NO. 143 NASSAU STREET.

The cover of the American Anti-Slavery Almanac for 1840 *illustrates the impossible situation that slaves faced at the time. Freed from the chains of the slave state—where slavery was legal—the slave is immediately bound in chains by the free state. This political cartoon refers to New York's nine months law, which allowed slaveholders from other states to enter the state with their slaves and remain for up to nine months. It was an exception to the state's otherwise antislavery legislation. The law was repealed in 1841.*

United States v. The Amistad

This detail from an 1837 broadside publication of an antislavery poem shows a slave on his knees, his outstretched arms bound in chains, above a banner pleading, "Am I not a man and a brother?" The picture was originally adopted as the seal of the Society for the Abolition of Slavery in England in the 1780s.

Because of the language barrier, finding a voice for the Africans was a challenge. Tappan and Leavitt knew they had to make the U.S. public more sympathetic toward the Africans. Being able to tell their story was one step closer to that goal. For example, one African named Konoma had very pronounced teeth that protruded out of his mouth. Those who were against the Africans claimed the teeth were used for eating human flesh. Konoma, however, said he thought his teeth made him more attractive to women.

Tappan began publishing descriptions of the Africans to change the ways Americans perceived them. Cinque had what many called a "noble air" about him. His picture was one of the most popular circulated in the United States. Through translators, Americans came to know him as a believer in a god who was good, and as one who believed in the truth.

After much difficulty, the committee tracked down local former slaves who were able to translate the words of the *Amistad* Africans into English. They learned from Cinque his life story, including his origins as the son of a prominent man in Africa who was abducted in exchange for his father's debt, bought by some Spaniards, and shipped to Cuba. Later, he described the brutal treatment onboard the *Amistad* and how he and the others tried to return home. Cinque was desperate to see his wife and three children.

Abolitionists and the Amistad Committee sent letters on behalf of the Africans to persons of political power, including President Martin Van Buren. Former president John Quincy Adams, now a member of the House of Representatives, heard much about the troubles and tribulations of the *Amistad* Africans. Although he was not formally an abolitionist, he believed that slavery stood contrary to the American ideals of liberty. He did not believe that President Van Buren would return the Africans to the Spanish.

The abolitionists decided to push the case into court. Little did they know what battles they would face.

District Court and Circuit Court

The history of legal decisions involving the Africans and the U.S. government began onboard the *Amistad* on August 28, following the capture of the ship by the U.S. Coast Guard. Judge Andrew T. Judson opened a hearing with the *Amistad* only a few yards away. After Judson examined the ship's papers, he heard the testimony of Ruiz and Montes, along with their request that the ship and its cargo, including the Africans, be handed over to the Spanish consul in Boston. Cinque and his companions were to be held until the next session of the United States circuit court in Hartford, Connecticut, on September 17. No one spoke for the Africans, and no one spoke to them either.

The court ruled against the Africans and decided that they should stand trial before the next circuit court. They were to be charged with murder and mutiny. The captives, now forty-four in number—including cabin boy Antonio and the girls, who were held as material witnesses—were then placed on a sloop to be transported to New Haven. Those who wished to possess the *Amistad*'s cargo hoped to have an easier time trying the case in Connecticut. In New Haven, the Africans were confined in jail. The children were not indicted, but bond was set at $100 to make sure they stayed in the United States as witnesses.

President Martin Van Buren is shown posing at his writing desk in this 1835 painting by Currier and Ives. Van Buren was known as "the Little Magician" because he was only five feet six, and because he was a crafty politician. He became the eighth president of the United States in 1832 and was the first president to be born on U.S. soil.

THE PRESIDENT APPEARS NEUTRAL

President Van Buren wanted little to do with the *Amistad* case. If he was perceived to favor the Africans in any way, his reelection would be in danger, and he did not want to anger his supporters in the slave-dependent South. Some historians argue that Van Buren did not consider a case involving slaves and a derelict ship to be very important. However, he felt it would be best to stay as far away from the case as possible and to end it as quickly as possible. Van Buren put the matter into the hands of Secretary of State John Forsyth. Forsyth was hardly objective. He was a slave owner from Georgia who had been a minister to Spain and favored the views of the Spanish minister.

Forsyth convinced the attorney general, Felix Grundy, and the rest of Van Buren's cabinet that Spain had the most legitimate claim to the *Amistad* cargo. William S. Holabird, the U.S. district attorney in Connecticut, was directed by Van Buren's cabinet to steer arguments about the case away from any U.S. jurisdiction. After all, the possible offenses involved citizens of a foreign state, took place on a foreign ship, and perhaps most important, occurred on the high seas, away from U.S. waters. Based on the Treaty of 1795, the United States had to "surrender" the case to the government of Spain.

A QUESTION OF PIRACY

But the question of piracy still remained. If the Africans had committed an act or acts of piracy, the United States would be bound by municipal and international law to try the case in U.S. courts. Grundy argued that the uprising on the *Amistad* was not an act of piracy because the matter was entirely Spanish in nature. He claimed that the Africans were not sailing the seas in search of cargo to plunder; they were considered by the law of nations to be property.

Since only individual countries could declare slavery to be illegal and Spain had not, the *Amistad* Africans were considered by Grundy and others to be property under Spanish rule. The *Amistad* was a Spanish vessel transporting Spanish property to a

Spanish port. Therefore, the United States could not take action and could not return the slaves to Africa. Based on this reasoning, President Van Buren had no option but to return the *Amistad* and its cargo to the queen of Spain. And then he could wash his hands clean of the matter.

This is a portrait of Marqu, also known as Margru, one of four Amistad children. In her native Africa, she was sold into slavery as payment for her father's debts. The drawing is by William H. Townsend and can be found at Yale University.

The abolitionists, including the friends of the Amistad Committee, prepared for the opening round of the trials by attempting to secure a writ of habeas corpus (a document requiring a physical body be brought to a trial) for the three African girls. The abolitionists hoped to show that no one could have legal claims on these children. If proven in a court of law, they felt the same reasoning would apply to rest of the adult *Amistad* prisoners and the boy. The trial would focus on the question of slavery and human rights. The abolitionists hoped the release and recognition of the *Amistad* Africans as free people would create similar feelings in the United States and bring about a swift end to slavery.

Large numbers of people attended the first hearing in the United States circuit court in Hartford, Connecticut.

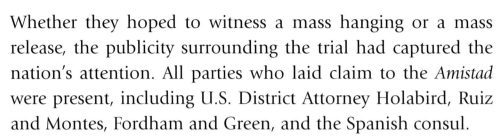

United States v. The Amistad

Whether they hoped to witness a mass hanging or a mass release, the publicity surrounding the trial had captured the nation's attention. All parties who laid claim to the *Amistad* were present, including U.S. District Attorney Holabird, Ruiz and Montes, Fordham and Green, and the Spanish consul.

The case was complicated enough to call into service two presiding judges, Associate Justice Smith Thompson from the Supreme Court and Andrew T. Judson from the district court. Lewis Tappan, Roger S. Baldwin, Seth P. Staples, and Theodore Sedgwick Jr. spoke for the Africans, arguing that they were illegally abducted from their homes in Africa, so no nation could make a claim on them.

The little girls had to be free, they argued, because they were obviously not born in the United States or Cuba. They did not meet the age requirements. More important, no charges had ever been brought against them, so they should never have been held at all.

CAN PEOPLE BE PROPERTY? CAN PROPERTY COMMIT CRIMES?

Baldwin limited his arguments to the question of property. Claims against the cargo of the *Amistad* were made, he argued, but in court stood people, not material objects. If the cargo of the *Amistad* was to be sold in Connecticut, they would have to establish a slave auction block. But Connecticut was a free state, so slaves could not be imported into the state. People were considered to be born free there. The Africans would have no value.

Those making claims on the Africans as slaves had to prove they were slaves. Since the men spoke African languages and did not know much English or Spanish, it was highly unlikely that they were born in English-speaking or Spanish-speaking colonies. Therefore, they could not be legally acquired slaves.

On September 23, Judge Thompson ruled that the case must be heard by the district court. Although the judge dropped the criminal charges against the Africans, it was not clear whether or not the *Amistad* Africans were slaves or free men.

At this point, the abolitionist lawyers again contacted former president John Quincy Adams and sought his help. Because of even greater attention paid to this case, Adams watched with greater interest. He even offered to aid the slaves. Eventually, he would become a primary voice in their defense.

To prepare for the next hearing, James Covey, a Mende from Africa and now a free man, heard the stories of the Africans and helped to prepare them to testify in court. Their stories were all the same. They told how they had been captured in Africa, and how they suffered great torture and brutality on the high seas. The details were all the same, including the humiliation of a slave auction in Havana, Cuba. From what the Africans told Covey, it was clear they were illegally enslaved. Now, their lawyers would have to prove that fact in court.

ILLEGAL AND LEGAL SLAVES

Following a delay in the proceedings, the district court finally met on January 7, 1840. The judge had already taken

JAMES COVEY, the interpreter for the Africans, is apparently about 20 years of age; was born at Benderi, in the Mendi country. His father was of Kon-no descent, and his mother Gissi. Covey was taken by three men, in the evening, from his parents' house, at Go-la-hung, whither they had removed when he was quite young. He was carried to the Bullom country, and sold as a slave to Ba-yi-mi, the king of the Bul-loms, who resided at Mani. He lived there for three years, and was employed to plant rice for the wife of Ba-yi-mi, who treated him with great kindness. He was sold to a Portuguese, living near Mani, who carried him, with 200 or 300 others to Lomboko, for the purpose of being transported to America. After staying in this place about one month, Covey was put on board a Portuguese slave-ship, which, after being out about four days from Lomboko, was captured by a British armed vessel, and carried into Sierra Leone. Covey thus obtained his freedom, and remained in this place five or six years, and was taught to read and write the English language, in the schools of the Church Missionary Society. Covey's original name was *Kaw-we-li*, which signifies, in Mendi, *war road*, i. e., a road dangerous to pass, for fear of being taken captive. His Christian name, James, was given him by Rev. J. W. Weeks, a Church Missionary, at Sierra Leone. In Nov., 1838, he enlisted as a sailor on board the British brig of war Buzzard, commanded by Captain Fitzgerald. It was on board this vessel, when at New York, in Oct., 1839, that James was found, amid some twenty native Africans, and by the kindness of captain Fitzgerald, his services as an interpreter were procured.

James Covey.

From John Warner Barber's 1840 book, A History of the Amistad Captives, *this illustration and short biography of James Covey was printed along with similar assessments of the* Amistad *slaves. Covey was captured as a boy and sold into slavery. A ship upon which he was being transported was taken over by the British, and he obtained his freedom and learned to read and write English. Enlisting as a sailor brought him to American shores. Covey became the chief interpreter for the* Amistad *prisoners.*

testimony from Dr. Richard R. Madden, an expert on the slave trade and contemporary Cuban attitudes toward slavery. Through conversations with the *Amistad* prisoners, Madden had no doubt that they were brought illegally into Cuba and he felt they should be returned to Africa. He also testified that thousands of illegal slaves, called *Bozales*, were brought into Cuba each year and that Spanish authorities did little to prevent it. In fact, many authorities signed false documents to establish the *Bozales* as *Ladinos* (legal slaves) and were paid for this service.

Madden's testimony had been reported in the press and captured the attention and anger of the Spanish minister, and finally, the sympathy of the queen of England. She wrote to the Spanish court and asked for the release of the prisoners and the arrest of Montes and Ruiz.

And the arrest did happen. Cinque and another prisoner, named Fuli, sued Montes and Ruiz for assault and battery and false imprisonment. The arrest of Montes and Ruiz stirred up the debate in the newspapers.

Judge Judson began to feel the pressure. Visitors from across the country, law students, representatives from foreign governments, claimants, numerous lawyers, and the *Amistad* prisoners filled his courtroom.

Based on the evidence presented on the first day of the trial, Judge Judson determined that the prisoners were indeed native Africans. Although this was the first major victory for the Africans, it did not necessarily guarantee their release. Baldwin's defense of liberty in his arguments for the Africans brought cheers throughout the courtroom.

At the trial, the strongest voice, perhaps, came from the African prisoners. Cinque was brought as a witness and told his story with the help of Covey as interpreter. First, Cinque was questioned about the events surrounding the Africans' arrest and capture. He narrated events from their capture up to the rebellion on the *Amistad*. Throughout his testimony, he emphasized the brutality of his captors.

Many other prisoners spoke that day, repeating what Cinque had said and adding important details, such as the murder of one of the Africans by Captain Ferrer.

Then the prosecution took over. District Attorney Holabird insisted the Africans made up the entire story and could not be trusted. He portrayed them as desperate murderers

United States v. The Amistad

These pencil sketches of Amistad *slaves were drawn from life by William H. Townsend while the Africans were being held in the United States. On the left is Grabo, who was second in command to Cinque. He was captured in Africa and enslaved in exchange for a debt owed by his uncle. In the center is Bar, who was captured on a road on his way to buy clothes. On the right is Kimbo. He was described by an interviewer as middle-aged and intelligent.*

who played off the sympathies of the abolitionists. Like Cinque, his passion for the case held sway in the courtroom.

ILLEGAL DOCUMENTS

A few days later, after the testimonies of lawyers and Antonio the cabin boy, and readings of statements by authorities, Baldwin gave his closing arguments. Following the leads of Sedgwick and Staples, Baldwin argued the inherent freedom of the Africans. They were born in Africa, illegally enslaved, and transported to countries that had outlawed the importation of slaves. The licenses that were previously recognized by the U.S. and Cuban governments had been proven as frauds. Therefore,

State of Connecticut
County of New Haven ss. New Haven, Oct 7, 1839

Kimbo, a colored man, deposeth and saith,
That he was born at Mankobah, a town of
Sauch-umah, in the Mendi country in Africa,
that he was sold to a Spaniard at Lomboko more
than six months ago, that he was brought from
Lomboko to Havanna more than six months ago,
that he was landed by night at a small village
near Havanna where he was kept five nights,
thence removed to another village where he was
kept five nights more, that he was then carried
by force on board the vessel in which he came to
this country; that on board the vessel he had
half enough to eat and drink, two potatoes and
one plantain twice a day, half a teacup of
water morning and evening; that asking for more
water, he was driven back with a whip, that the
Spaniards washed their own clothes in fresh water;
that for stealing some water he received a severe
beating, that he was held down over a piece
of timber, and beaten with twenty three lashes on
the back, that this was done by Pipi, who bought
him (his master) the cook, Antonio, and another
uniting; that this flogging was repeated morning
and evening two days, that powder and rum
were applied to his wounds, that Pipi told he

Pictured above is an affidavit created from testimony given by Amistad slave Kimbo to Lewis Tappan, with James Covey interpreting. The transcript is from 1839 and is housed in the Library of Congress. Kimbo's account includes the story of being beaten for attempting to steal fresh water: "[H]e was held down over a piece of lumber, and beaten with twenty-three lashes on the back . . ."

when officials of the U.S. government captured them off Long Island, the Africans were free.

Judge Judson waited until the following Monday to make his ruling. Outside the New Haven harbor sat two ships: The *Grampus* waited to take the Africans back to Cuba; an unnamed ship hired by the abolitionist Anti-Slavery Society was to take the prisoners back to Africa.

After intense testimony and pressure, the judge was ready to rule. On January 13, 1840, Judge Judson ruled:

1. When the *Amistad* was seized, it was on, for all practical purposes, high seas. The district court had the right to rule in the matter;

2. Gedney and Meade had performed their duties and were entitled to salvage equal to one-third the total value, excepting the *Amistad* prisoners;

3. The Spanish government could make salvage claims on the ship itself, but as to the Africans, there was no way to place a value. Slavery was illegal in Connecticut, so their value was nothing. Montes and Ruiz had no claims. Judge Judson suggested that Ruiz and Montes find the man who sold them the slaves to get their money back;

4. Green and Fordham had no legitimate claims and were not entitled to any properties or monies resulting from the salvage of the *Amistad*.

More important, Judge Judson ruled that the Africans aboard the *Amistad* were illegally enslaved. The United States would not return them to the condition of slavery, based on laws passed in 1819. The judge said that the Africans "shall not sigh for Africa in vain. Bloody as may be their hands, they shall yet embrace their kindred." He concluded that they would be delivered to the president of the United States, who would be bound to return them to Africa. Only Antonio, who was legally enslaved, and the estate of Ferrer, the captain of the *Amistad* who was killed during the uprising, would be returned to Cuba.

VICTORY, BUT NO SUCCESS

One would have to assume the *Amistad* case was over and the freedom of the Africans was guaranteed by the courts and due process. Overall, it was a surprising verdict because Judge Judson had long been considered an enemy of the abolitionist movement.

A

HISTORY

OF THE

AMISTAD CAPTIVES:

BEING A

CIRCUMSTANTIAL ACCOUNT

OF THE

CAPTURE OF THE SPANISH SCHOONER AMISTAD,

BY THE AFRICANS ON BOARD;

THEIR VOYAGE, AND CAPTURE

NEAR LONG ISLAND, NEW YORK; WITH

BIOGRAPHICAL SKETCHES

OF EACH OF THE SURVIVING AFRICANS

ALSO, AN ACCOUNT OF

THE TRIALS

HAD ON THEIR CASE, BEFORE THE DISTRICT AND CIRCUIT COURTS OF THE
UNITED STATES, FOR THE DISTRICT OF CONNECTICUT.

COMPILED FROM AUTHENTIC SOURCES,

BY JOHN W. BARBER,
MEM. OF THE CONNECTICUT HIST. SOC.

NEW HAVEN, CT.:
PUBLISHED BY E. L. & J. W. BARBER.
HITCHCOCK & STAFFORD, PRINTERS.

1840.

In 1840, John W. Barber published *A History of the Amistad Captives*. *The book included biographical sketches of the slaves and the story of their journey, rebellion, imprisonment, and trial. The book is part of the African American Odyssey in the Library of Congress.*

One would also assume that the abolitionists who aided the *Amistad* Africans would have felt this to be a total victory. But they did not. The judge did not rule that blacks or Africans had the same rights as white people—as was their hope. The abolitionists wanted this case to serve as a precedent (example) for the abolition of slavery.

Before the judgment, Secretary of State Forsyth had the *Grampus* in shipshape, ready to sail the prisoners back to Cuba. After the verdict, he had Holabird appeal the decision. Because of intense pressure regarding international relations with Spain and the way the verdict would be received in the South, the president of the United States would not let this decision stand. The case now moved to the Supreme Court.

Forged in the Fires of Adversity

4

That President Van Buren would direct his cabinet and lawyers to appeal the case to the Supreme Court clearly stated his position on the question of slavery in the United States. He hoped to be reelected that year and saw his success in this case as a way to define his presidency in history. Certainly, the case of the *United States v. the Amistad* did. However, a former president, John Quincy Adams, solidified his place in U.S. history as a champion of civil liberties.

Adams lived in the shadow of his more famous father, John Adams, patriot, philosopher, first vice president of the United States, and second president of the United States. "People and nations are forged in the fires of adversity," his famous father said, and this would prove to be true for his son. As a youth, he witnessed firsthand the Battle of Bunker Hill and legions of U.S. statesmen who came through the door of his house. Thomas Jefferson, the author of the

United States v. The Amistad

This hand-colored lithograph of John Quincy Adams was created by E. B. & E. C. Kellogg around 1848. Adams had a long career in politics—including being the sixth president of the United States—before defending the Amistad Africans. The portrait resides in the Library of Congress Prints and Photographs Division.

Declaration of Independence, was a great influence on the young Adams.

John Quincy Adams served as secretary of state under President James Monroe and helped to develop the famous Monroe Doctrine. As president, Adams supported a canal system to link various parts of the United States together. This is important because one can see early on the vision of Adams, who believed that the states should indeed be united. He also supported the establishment of a national university devoted to scientific development and the arts, which would put the young nation in a position of world leadership. Now, for the *Amistad* prisoners, his leadership would be greatly needed.

Adams called Van Buren's orders to ship the Africans back to Cuba on the *Grampus* lawless and tyrannical, and from his position in the House of Representatives asked that all official documents regarding this case be reviewed by members of Congress and then made public.

House Document 185, the printed record of the official documents pertaining to the case of the *Amistad*, clearly revealed a president who may have abused his powers by influencing the judicial system and by ordering the *Grampus* to take the Africans back to Cuba.

THE CASE GOES TO THE SUPREME COURT

Nearly a year after the decision in district court, the *Amistad* case went before the Supreme Court. During that time, Van Buren's attempts to extend his presidency failed. William Henry Harrison defeated him.

Abolitionists did everything they could to raise defense funds and to sway public opinion in favor of the Africans. The lawyers spent large amounts of time narrowing their focus for the defense. Baldwin and Adams would need to reprove the case of the Africans. Adams, seventy years old and in questionable health, had not argued a case before the Supreme Court in thirty years. However, he had acquired the nickname "Old Man Eloquent."

Waiting for the case to come before the Supreme Court was extremely difficult for the *Amistad* prisoners. They had been attending classes and had learned some English. This allowed them some understanding of the complexity of their case, but the knowledge increased their frustration.

Adding to their discomfort was spending time in the brutal cold of another New England winter. They had already been through so much emotional and physical upheaval. Many did not know how they would survive if they did not win the Supreme Court case. Their bodies and their spirits

United States v. The Amistad

THE SUPREME COURT

The Supreme Court is the highest court in the land. Justices are chosen by presidential appointment and congressional confirmation. Decisions rendered by the Court are considered final. The justices interpret the law based on the Constitution of the United States of America. One judge sits as chief justice and eight others (their number having been determined by Congress) are associate judges. The building that houses the Supreme Court is in Washington, D.C.

Cases go to the Supreme Court when the lower courts are unable to reach a final, satisfactory decision. There is no jury for cases tried in the Supreme Court, and witnesses are never heard. The Supreme Court justices review cases to determine which are appropriate for a Supreme Court decision.

Each member of the Supreme Court votes in every case, unless he or she cannot be impartial on the matter. The final outcome is determined by the vote count.

were distressed. Most had been imprisoned in the Pendletons' jail for nearly two years.

They were heartened by visits from Adams and the tireless efforts of their supporters. Many had embraced Christianity and were comforted by the spiritual nature of the religion.

Forged in the Fires of Adversity

At that time, the Supreme Court of the United States had upheld proslavery decisions based on the continuing struggle to retain states' rights. Adams doubted his ability to convince the justices to release the *Amistad* captives.

THE ARGUMENTS

On February 22, 1841, both sides presented their opening arguments. Sitting before them was Chief Justice Roger B. Taney (Maryland) and associate justices John Catron (Tennessee), John McKinley (Alabama), Joseph Story (Massachusetts), Smith Thompson (New York), John McLean (Ohio), Henry Baldwin (Pennsylvania), James M. Wayne (Georgia), and Philip P. Barbour (Virginia).

Chief Justice Roger B. Taney (1777–1864) was the fifth chief justice in U.S. Supreme Court history. Taney was born to a family of slave owners and advocated the practice of slavery throughout his career. This official Supreme Court portrait was painted by George P. Healey and is housed in the collection of the Supreme Court.

Speaking on behalf of the United States, Attorney General Henry Gilpin tried to emphasize two main points. His first was that the papers proving the *Amistad* Africans were illegal slaves were fraudulent; therefore, under the conditions of the Treaty of 1795, the Africans were slaves, were property, and ought to be returned. His second argument involved the legality of all the

United States v. The Amistad

In the matter of the United States Appellants

vs

Sinque and others severally claimants and appellees

J. Q. Adams, of Counsel for the said Africans, moves the Court for a certiorari to the Judge of the Circuit and District Court of the United States, for the District of Connecticut, to amend the Record of the proceedings in the said District and Circuit Courts in this case, by sending up copies of the following papers.

1. The proceedings of the Court of Enquiry holden by the honourable Judge of the District Court on board the Schooner Amistad on the 29th of August 1839, and particularly the Indictment against the said Africans for the murder of the captain and mate or cook of the said Schooner. The warrant of seizure issued by the said District Judge on the said 29th of August 1839. directed to the Marshal of the said District, together with the monitions and other process according to Law and the return made by the said Marshal made on the 30th of august aforesaid to the said warrant of seizure; and the return to the said monitions.

2. The two warrants of seizure issued by the said District Judge on the 18th of September 1839 and the returns of the Marshal thereon — with the process of monition and returns thereon.

John Quincy Adams's request for papers from the Amistad's lower court trials is shown above. The document was written on January 23, 1841. Adams used the papers to prepare for his appearance in court, where, for over eight hours, he defended the slaves' right to freedom. The document is part of the U.S. National Archives and Records Administration in Washington, D.C.

action taken to secure the return of the *Amistad* back to Spain. He cited previous cases, and argued that the case of the *United States v. The Amistad* was quite similar. The United States should return the *Amistad* and all its cargo to Spain. Essentially, the arguments against the *Amistad* Africans were the same as presented in the lower courts. Then, it was Baldwin's turn.

Baldwin opened his arguments before the Supreme Court by reminding the Court it had already been proven that the defendants had been born free, kidnapped in Africa, transported illegally across the Atlantic, illegally sold in Cuba, and found near Culloden Point in New York, a state that outlawed slavery. Also, their removal from New York to Connecticut was illegal. If the United States decided against the Africans, then it would be guilty of enslaving freeborn Africans.

By the law of the 1795 treaty, the Spanish government, he said, had more than a year to prove ownership of the *Amistad* Africans. They had failed. The only thing left to do was to return the Africans to their home.

OLD MAN ELOQUENT

After the second day, Adams took over. The case became personal for him. During the months of preparation for the case, he had corresponded with many of the prisoners and found their passion and humanity inspiring. He would use their words and ideals in his arguments for their defense. He sympathized with their situation onboard the *Amistad*, "The Africans were in possession, and had the presumptive right of ownership; they were in peace with the United States; the Courts have decided, and truly, that they were not pirates; they were on a voyage to their native homes . . . "

United States v. The Amistad

Painted by muralist Hale Woodruff, the above scene is entitled, The Trial Scene of the Amistad Captives. *The painting was unveiled in 1939 and is now located in the Savery Library, Talladega College, in Talladega, Alabama. Hale created three panels about the* Amistad *story:* The Mutiny *and* Return to Mendeland *completed the series.*

After recounting the death toll suffered by the *Amistad* Africans, he sympathized with their conditions as enslaved and what he determined to be illegally imprisoned:

> Although placed in a condition which, if applied to forty citizens of the United States, we should call cruel, shut up eighteen months in a prison, and enjoying only the tenderness which our laws provide for the worst of criminals, so great is the improvement of their condition from what it was in the hands of Ruiz, that they have perfectly recovered

their health, and not one has died; when, before that time, they were perishing from hour to hour.

Because Adams had been secretary of state in 1819, the year the Treaty of 1795 was renewed, he had firsthand knowledge of the meaning of the treaty. He said with certainty that neither the United States nor Spain meant to include human beings within the definition of property.

In his interpretation of the Treaty of 1795 for the Supreme Court, Adams illuminated one of the supreme contradictions of the condition of slavery. If the *Amistad* Africans were indeed "merchandise" or "property," then how could they steal themselves?

But my clients are claimed under the treaty as merchandise, rescued from pirates and robbers. Who were the merchandise, and who were the robbers? According to the construction of the Spanish minister, the merchandise were the robbers, and the robbers were the merchandise. The merchandise was rescued out of its own hands, and the robbers were rescued out of the hands of the robbers. Is this the meaning of the treaty?

He continued his argument:

Is any thing more absurd than to say these forty Africans are robbers, out of whose hands they have themselves been rescued? Can a greater absurdity be imagined in construction than this, which applies the double character of robbers and of merchandise to human beings?

He referred to a copy of the Declaration of Independence, hanging on a column in the courtroom. The ideals of Thomas Jefferson—"unalienable rights" to "life, liberty, and the pursuit of happiness"—applied to the Africans as well, he argued. "I know of no other law that reaches my clients," he said, "but the law of Nature and of Nature's God on which our fathers placed our national existence."

He then attacked the former president, Van Buren, implying that secret communication with the Spanish minister and the Spanish government interfered with the right of due process. He said that Van Buren's motives were political, for his own benefit, and did nothing to advance the pursuit of liberty. He used powerful language, calling certain actions nothing short of conspiracy. By most accounts, his arguments were very emotional.

When the Court resumed the next day, Justice Philip P. Barbour was not present. He had died the previous evening. The Court went into recess until March 1.

THE FINAL RULING

When the trial resumed, Adams noticed the Court seemed impatient with his defense. He, too, was very tired. To conclude, Adams used this case as a way to say good-bye and end his career as a lawyer. This, he thought, would be his final appearance before the Supreme Court. He recalled his previous appearances before the Court, friends and colleagues who had heard his arguments decades before in the Supreme Court. He pointed out the fact that he was the lone survivor. He asked for God's blessings on the Court and hoped that when their work was done, and they entered heaven, they would hear, "Well done, good and faithful servant; enter thou into the joy of thy Lord." The moral tone of his final message underscored his entire defense of the *Amistad* Africans.

That defense centered on the idea that it was the Supreme Court's moral responsibility to uphold the principles of freedom. He and Baldwin both argued that the Supreme Court did not have any jurisdiction in the case, and that the Supreme Court must uphold the previous ruling in district court.

Against the odds, the Supreme Court did exactly that. On March 9, 1841, Chief Justice Robert B. Taney declared the *Amistad* Africans free. However, their journey was not over.

Free, But Not Home

5

The Africans were finally free. The Supreme Court decision was ultimately final, but the controversy was far from over. Appeals in this case continued until President Abraham Lincoln's administration in 1860. But as Justice Joseph Story said, the Africans' rebellion aboard the *Amistad* was a just action, as an "ultimate right of all human beings in extreme cases to resist oppression, and to apply force against ruinous injustice."

The problem with the decision for the abolitionists was that the Supreme Court decision applied only to those who were born free. The case of *United States v. The Amistad* did not end slavery in the United States as the abolitionists hoped it might. In some ways, it confirmed the overwhelming futility for those born in slavery—they would not be free unless their masters decided to release them.

As an institution, slavery was not seen as immoral or against God. The Supreme Court had based its decision on the fact that the U.S. attorneys could not prove legal ownership of the Africans as slaves. As persons born free, the Africans were released.

Now the problem arose as to what to do with the freed Africans.

HOW TO GET HOME?

With the dismissal of the case, the Amistads, as they were now called, were responsible for their own return to Africa.

Housed in the National Portrait Gallery, this 1827 oil painting of Justice Joseph Story was painted by Chester Harding. Story delivered the Court's opinion on the Amistad case. Although Story often voted to uphold slavery, he believed the Amistad slaves should be freed.

Abolitionists, friends of the Amistad Committee members, and the Union Missionary Society needed to raise funds to send the Amistads back to their homes in Sierra Leone, West Africa.

Many of the *Amistad* supporters, however, were not anxious to send the Africans home. The Amistads drew huge crowds in public-speaking engagements. They were still a topic of popular discussion. Abolitionists and missionaries saw the Amistads as a way to popularize their ambitious reform movement.

United States v. The Amistad

November 19, 1841

The Subscribers, Committee on behalf of the Africans of the Amistad, now preparing to send them to Sierra Leone, and to Mendi, solicit of the friends of these injured men such provisions and other articles as they are disposed to give Joseph L. Chester agent on behalf of the Committee

New York Nov. 19: 1841

S. S. Jocelyn

Lewis Tappan

This letter was written by Lewis Tappan and Simeon Jocelyn on November 19, 1841, in New York City. It was sent out to solicit provisions to give the Amistad Africans for their journey home. The men suggested donations of clothing, shoes, fabric, cash, and food. This document is housed in the Amistad Research Center.

What did the Africans think of their new freedom? To most, it seemed another form of captivity. While many enjoyed the benefits of education (they were being trained as missionaries) and a certain level of popularity, they toiled hard on a farm in Farmington, Connecticut, producing food for their journey home. They became even more depressed and angry because the freedom they sought and fought for was not yet a reality.

One of them, Fawni, suffered an untimely death. He drowned while swimming in one of the farm ponds. Many of the Africans wondered how a man known as an excellent swimmer could drown. As told by those who knew him, Fawni had been extremely depressed by how long it was taking them to get home. Did homesickness lead him to suicide?

What became of the children? The three girls were left in the care of the Pendeltons, the New Haven couple who once sold tickets to see the prisoners. In effect, the Pendletons were keeping the girls as slaves. When the case was taken to court, the girls testified that they wanted to stay with the Pendletons because they were told they would be sold back into slavery if they didn't stay. They were moved to a temporary

Considered by many to be extreme, Lewis Tappan (1788–1873) advocated interracial marriages and procreations so that race would no longer be an issue in America. He was persecuted for his ideals. Scare tactics included death threats and harrassment, including a rope and a slave's ear sent to him through the mail.

home, where they lived until the Amistads could return home.

The cabin boy, Antonio, legally proven as property of Captain Ferrer's heirs, also ended up in the Pendleton household. He disappeared, and an angry Spanish government accused the abolitionists of freeing him through the Underground Railroad.

AFRICA!

After Fawni's death, the abolitionists realized they needed to dedicate their efforts solely toward the Africans' journey

United States v. The Amistad

Farmington. May. 5th. 1841.

Mr John Q. Adams

Dear Friend

We thank you very much because you make us free & because you love all Mendi people. They give you money for Mendi people & you say you will not take it, because you love Mendi people. We love you very much & we will pray for you when we rise upon the morning & when we lie down at night. We hope the Lord will love you very much & take you up to heaven when you die. We pray for all the good people who make us free. Wicked people want to make us slaves but the Great God who has made all things made up friends for Mendi people. We begin us Mr Adams that he may make me free & all Mendi people free Mr Adams we write our names for you. Kali.

Mr Adams

Dear friend. We write this to you because you plead with the Great Court to make us free and now we are free and joyful we thank the Great God. I hope God will bless you dear friend. Mendi people will remember you when we go to our own country & we will tell our friends about you and we will say to them Mr Adams is a great man and he plead for us and how very glad we be and our friends will love you very much because you was a very good man and oh how joyful we shall be. We hope the great God will send down his Holy Spirit

The document beginning above and ending on the next page was sent to John Quincy Adams from the Amistad slaves on May 5, 1841. Three of the Amistads wrote gracious notes thanking Adams for helping them obtain freedom. The other slaves signed their names to the bottom of the page. "Some cannot write," the letter concludes, "so we write for them." The document is kept at the Amistad Research Center.

upon you and have mercy upon you & that our dear Saviour Jesy Christ will bless you & give you a new heart. We write this because you plead for us. We give you good love.

Kinna.

Dear Friend I desire to write you a letter because you be so kind to poor Mendi people. Dear Friend I call you my brother because you set us Free. Mendi people thank you very much and we will pray for you every day and night that God will keep you from danger. Dear sir who make you become great President over America people God - God make every thing. He make men to do good and love one another.

your Friend Foole.

Mr Adams We write our names for you in this Bible that you may remember Mendi People. Some cannot write so we write for them.

Kali   Cinque   Cici   Kinna Faliama
Banna   Fagino Bata

home. The thirty-five surviving adults and three girls set sail on a ship, the *Gentleman*, on November 27, 1841. Their destination: home. By mid-January of 1842, they finally arrived.

Home was not the same place as when they left. Wars and slave raids had killed, wounded, or made captives of many of their families. For some, their villages did not exist anymore. Some became missionaries in West Africa and kept in contact with their missionary friends in the United States.

What happened to Cinque is nearly as mysterious as the black schooner that started this story. Historians know that Cinque returned to his village only to find out that his

United States v. The Amistad

The Freedom Schooner Amistad, *a reproduction of the original Spanish schooner, is owned and operated by AMISTAD America, Inc., a nonprofit educational organization. The ship travels nationally and internationally to serve as a floating classroom and a monument to the* Amistad *incident. Its home port is the Long Wharf Pier in New Haven, Connecticut.*

entire family had been killed or captured as slaves. Stories differ as to what he did after that. It is known that he tried to help missionaries in Freetown and York, but he soon left after that. In *Amistad: The Slave Uprising Aboard the Spanish Schooner*, Helen Kromer reports that Cinque could have been an interpreter, a chief among his people, and possibly became a slave trader himself. It has also been suggested that he traveled to the West Indies, lived there for several years, and returned to West Africa shortly before his death.

THE EFFECTS OF THE *AMISTAD*

The tale of the *Amistad* is one that stretches far past the historical dates of rebellion and trials. For many of the enslaved Africans in the United States, the story of the *Amistad* rebellion inspired rebellions in slave-holding states. For the abolitionist movement, the rebellion sparked a national debate over slavery and fueled the eventual liberation of all enslaved in the United States. The various committees and alliances formed around the case of *United States v. The Amistad* remained long after the trial was over. One of those groups, the American Missionary Association, devoted great energy to the cause of education and eventually moved into the South. More than five hundred black schools and colleges are part of the legacy.

During the Harlem Renaissance of the 1920s, the *Amistad* was a popular theme for artists and intellectuals. During the Black Arts movement and the Civil Rights movement of the 1960s, the *Amistad* case was important as a symbol of rebellion. Numerous poems, plays, songs, and other works of art by African Americans reflect the positive inspiration of the Amistads.

As we look back on this event from a twenty-first-century perspective, those Africans who decided that slavery was death for them, that they would rather risk their lives for freedom, are indeed heroes. They took up arms against their captors, and their case was found just in the highest court of a foreign land. Their sacrifices and their impact are immeasurable.

Glossary

abolitionist A person whose goal was to permanently free all those enslaved and to bring about the end of slavery forever.

appeal The transfer of a case from a lower to a higher court for a new hearing.

civil liberties Fundamental individual rights.

futility Uselessness.

indicted Formally charged.

inherent Permanently existing in something or someone.

liberty Freedom.

mutiny Rebellion against authority, often by the sailors on a ship.

pirate A person who illegally captures ships and seizes their cargo for profit, usually committing murder among other crimes to do so.

rights of salvage A claim of property based on the right to take control of a vessel so distressed it cannot remain safely on the seas.

schooner A small sailing vessel with two masts.

Underground Railroad A secret network that helped slaves reach freedom.

uprising A revolt against a government.

For More Information

AMISTAD America, Inc.

746 Chapel Street, Suite 300

New Haven, CT 06510

(203) 495-1839

Web site: http://www.amistadamerica.org

The Amistad Research Center

Tilton Hall—Tulane University

6823 St. Charles Avenue

New Orleans, LA 70118

(504) 865 5535

Web site: http://www.tulane.edu/~amistad

Web Sites

Due to the changing nature of Internet links, the Rosen Publishing Group, Inc., has developed an online list of Web sites related to the subject of this book. This site is updated regularly. Please use this link to access the list:

http://www.rosenlinks.com/scctps/unsa

For Further Reading

Chambers, Veronica. *Amistad Rising: A Story of Freedom.* New York: Harcourt, 1998.

Jurmain, Suzanne. *Freedom's Sons: The True Story of the Amistad Mutiny.* New York: William Morrow & Co., 1998.

Myers, Walter Dean. *Amistad: A Long Road to Freedom.* New York: Penguin Putnam, 1998.

Worth, Richard. *Cinque of the Amistad and the Slave Trade in World History.* Berkeley Heights, NJ: Enslow Publishers, Inc., 2001.

Zeinert, Karen. *The Amistad Slave Revolt and American Abolition.* North Haven, CT: Shoe String Press, 1997.

Bibliography

"The *Amistad* Case: The Arguments of John Quincy Adams Before the Supreme Court." Retrieved October 2002 (http://www.multied.com/amistad/amistad.html).

Amistad Research Center. Retrieved November 2002 (http://www.tulane.edu/~amistad).

Cable, Mary. *Black Odyssey*. New York: Viking, 1971.

Franklin, John Hope, and Alfred A. Moss Jr. *From Slavery to Freedom: A History of Negro Americans*. New York: Alfred A Knopf, 1988.

Hoyt, Edwin P. The *Amistad Affair*. London: Abelard-Schuman, 1970.

Huggins, Nathan Irvin. *Black Odyssey: The Afro-American Ordeal in Slavery*. New York: Vintage, 1977.

Jones, Howard. *Mutiny on the Amistad*. New York: Oxford University Press, Inc., 1987.

Kromer, Helen. *Amistad: The Slave Uprising Aboard the Spanish Schooner*. Cleveland: The Pilgrim Press, 1997.

Martin, B. Edmon. *All We Want Is Make Us Free: La Amistad and the Reform Abolitionists*. Lanham, MD: University Press of America, 1986.

Primary Source Image List

Cover: Illustrated print, *Death of Captain Ferrer, the Captain of the Amistad*, July 1839. Created in 1839 for John W. Barber's book, *A History of the Amistad Captives*.

Page 5: *La Amistad* watercolor by an unknown artist, dating from the nineteenth century. Housed in the New Haven Colony Historical Society.

Page 8: Painting of slaves arriving in Jamestown, Virginia. Painted by Howard Pyle in 1917. Published in *Harper's Weekly* in 1917.

Page 9: Portrait of Cinque, painted by Simeon Jocelyn in 1839. Housed in the New Haven Colony Historical Society.

Page 12: Wood engraving of *Amistad* men wrestling. Illustrated in 1913 by Irving L. Hurlbert. Housed in the Library of Congress.

Page 16: Photograph of Wilson Chinn. Taken by Kimball in 1863. Housed in the Library of Congress.

Page 17: Woodcut of iron mask and collar. Published in Thomas Branagan's book, *The Penitential Tyrant* in 1807. Housed in the Library of Congress Rare Book and Special Collections Division.

Page 19: Wood engraving of a slave auction. Published in the *Illustrated London News* on September 27, 1856. Kept in the Library of Congress Prints and Photographs Division.

Page 21: Cover of *American Anti-Slavery Almanac* for 1840. Printed in New York in 1840.

Page 22: Woodcut *Am I Not a Man and a Brother?* Appearing on the 1837 broadside publication of John Greenleaf Whittier's poem, "Our Countrymen in Chains." Housed in the Library of Congress.

Page 25: Portrait of Martin Van Buren. Created by Currier and Ives in 1835. Housed in the Library of Congress.

Page 27: Illustration of Marqu. Drawn by William H. Townsend circa 1840. Housed in the Beinecke Rare Book and Manuscript Library, Yale University.

Page 31: Illustration of James Covey. Taken from page 15 of John Warner Barber's 1840 book *A History of the Amistad Captives*.

Page 32: Illustrations of Grabo, Bar, and Kimbo. Drawn by William H. Townsend circa 1840. Housed in the Beinecke Rare Book and Manuscript Library, Yale University.

Page 33: Affidavit of Kimbo, from the Lewis Tappan papers. Created in 1839. Housed in the Library of Congress.

Page 35: Cover of *A History of the Amistad Captives*. Written by John W. Barber in 1840. Housed in the Library of Congress.

Page 38: Hand-colored lithograph of John Quincy Adams. Created by E. B. & E.

C. Kellogg circa 1848. Housed in the Library of Congress Prints and Photographs Division.

Page 41: Portrait of Roger Taney. Painted by George P. Healy. Housed in the Collection of the Supreme Court of the United States.

Page 42: Letter from John Quincy Adams requesting documents. Written on January 23, 1841. Housed in the U.S. National Archives and Records Administration.

Page 44-45: *The Trial Scene of the Amistad Captives*. Painted by Hale Woodruff. Unveiled in 1939. Housed in the Savery Library, Talladega College, in Talladega, Alabama.

Page 49: Portrait of Joseph Story. Oil on canvas, painted by Chester Harding in 1827. Part of the permanent collection of the National Portrait Gallery, Smithsonian Institution in Washington, D.C.

Page 50: Letter to the subscribers committee from Lewis Tappan and Simeon Jocelyn. Written on November 19, 1941 in New York City. Located in The Amistad Research Center, Tulane University.

Page 51: Portrait of Lewis Tappan. Painted circa 1840.

Page 52: Letter from *Amistad* slaves to John Quincy Adams. Written on May 5, 1841, in Farmington, Connecticut. Located in The Amistad Research Center, Tulane University.

Page 54: Photograph of *Freedom Schooner Amistad*. The reproduction was launched in 2000 and resides in New Haven, Connecticut's Long Wharf Pier.

Index

About the Author

David Hulm is a college instructor, freelance writer, poet, and father of a wonderful daughter.

Photo Credits

Eagle on back cover and throughout interior © Eyewire; Red curtain throughout interior © Arthur S. Aubry/PhotoDisc; Wood grain on cover and back cover and throughout interior © M. Angelo/Corbis; Cover, pp. 30, 35 Library of Congress General Collections; pp. 5, 9 © AP/Wide World Photos; p. 8 © CORBIS; pp. 12, 16, 19, 38 Library of Congress Prints and Photographs Division; pp. 17, 22, 25 Library of Congress Rare Book and Special Collections Division; pp. 21, 51 © Hulton/Archive/Getty Images; pp. 27, 32 Beinecke Rare Book and Manuscript Library, Yale University; p. 33 Library of Congress Manuscript Division; p. 41 Painting by George P. Healey, Collection of the Supreme Court of the United States; p. 42 National Archives and Records Administration; pp. 44–45 Savery Library Archives, Talladega College, Talladega, Alabama; p. 49 National Portrait Gallery, Smithsonian Institution, Washington, D.C./ Art Resource, NY; pp. 50, 52, 53 Amistad Research Center at Tulane University, New Orleans, LA; p. 54 Thomas P. Benincas Jr./New England Photo.

Designer: Evelyn Horovicz; Editor: Christine Poolos; Photo Researcher: Amy Feinberg